WHAT COMES

ON THE PAGE

BEFORE ME?

BY KRISTIN LEWIS

This book is dedicated to Jauan and Korinne. May you be inspired and dare to be true to thine own-self.

Nothing is on the page before me.

It is blank can't you see?

There is 1 yellow duck on the page before me. Can't you see?

There are 2 yellow ducks on the page before me. Can't you see?

There are 3 yellow ducks on the page before me. Can't you see?

There are 4 yellow ducks on the

page before me . Can't you see?

12

There are 5 yellow ducks on the

page before me. Can't you see?

14

There are 6 yellow ducks on the page before me. Can't you see?

16

There are 7 yellow ducks on the page before me. Can't you see?

18

There are 8 yellow ducks on the page before me. Can't you see?

There are 9 yellow ducks on the page before me. Can't you see?

There are 10 yellow ducks on the page before me. Can't you see?

There is nothing on the page before me. There is nothing on the page after me. We have counted the ducks. Can't you see?

The End

About the Author

Kristin Lewis was born and raised in Philadelphia, Pennsylvania. Kristin is an author, wife, and mother of two. Her passion for the youth was birthed out of her life experiences. In her early career, while serving as a Family Advocate, Kristin began her advocacy for at-risk youth by forming partnerships with parents and guardians in order to promote self-sufficiency.

Although Kristin's employment endeavors attributed to her desire to assist the youth and their families, it was her own childhood experiences that sparked a zeal of encouragement for others.

Kristin obtained a Bachelor of Arts in Psychology from Temple University and has made it her passion to produce literature that is engaging while promoting cognitive and social development.

For more about Kristin, visit her website at Breakthroughforme.com, like her Facebook page at www.facebook.com/authorklewis or follow her on Instagram @kristhechosen1

29